# If They Be Prophets...

# If They Be Prophets...

*

*Rediscovering the Ministry of the Prophet in the
New Testament Church*

**Written by: Roderick L. Evans**

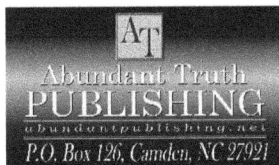

Aᴛ
Abundant Truth
PUBLISHING
abundantpublishing.net
P.O. Box 126, Camden, NC 27921

**If They Be Prophets...**
*Rediscovering the Ministry of the Prophet in the New Testament Church*

All Rights Reserved ©2019 by Roderick L. Evans

Front & Back Cover Designs by Abundant Truth
Publishing
www.sxc.hu

Abudant Truth Publishing
an imprint of Abundant Truth International Ministries

For information address:
Abundant Truth International
P.O. Box 126
Camden, NC 27921

**Unless otherwise indicated, all of the scripture quotations are taken from the** *Authorized King James Version* **of the Bible. Scripture quotations marked with NIV are taken from the** *New International Version* **of the Bible. Scripture quotations marked with NASV are taken from the** *New American Standard Version* **of the Bible. Scripture quotations marked with Amplified are taken from the** *Amplified Bible.*

ISBN: 978-1-60141-299-7

Printed in the United States of America

# *Contents*

# *Preface*

Prophets and prophetic ministry are important to the furtherance of the Kingdom of God and the Church. It is my prayer that the information presented in this work will bring clarity, appreciation, and understanding to prophets and prophetic ministry.

Numerous works have been produced which highlight the ministry of the prophet. This book is to be used in connection with other publications. It is our prayer that those called to this office will gain insight for their ministries. In addition, I pray that others will develop an understanding of this ministry in the Church.

*Roderick L. Evans*

# *Introduction*

Controversy over the gifts and ministries of the Spirit has abounded for centuries. Various scholars have taught that there was a cessation of the gifts and ministries. More specifically, they affirm that the ministry of the Prophet is no longer in operation nor valid. However, in recent years, a resurgence of the operation and demonstration of this ministry occurred. Traditional and Non-traditional churches, alike, have experienced the visitation of God through the Holy Spirit.

Since the emergence and acceptance of the ministries and gifts of the Holy Spirit, various authors have written concerning this phenomenon. In spite of this, many in the Church, presently, do not understand the functions and operations of, namely, the office of the Prophet. Even in organizations and denominations that consider this ministry valid today, comprehension is oftentimes elementary.

Where there is no clear understanding, individuals become vulnerable to deception and error. Since the prophetic office has authority and responsibility in the Kingdom of God, there are individuals in the Church who desire to function in this office.

There are men and women who know they are not called to this office, yet they pursue it. They lust after the respect that men have for those in this office. If they cannot be recognized as a prophet, some want to be identified with the office. Therefore, individuals resort to saying that they have a prophetic anointing upon their lives, without having any knowledge or understanding of the office or the anointing associated with it.

In this book, we will bring clarity to the role of the prophet in the New Testament Church. In addition, we will explain with simplicity the prophetic anointing. It is our prayer that believers will recognize the operation of this anointing in their lives and in the lives of others. We can be confident that God is still using His people in these last days.

# 1

# *What is a Prophet?*

The prophets are here! God always spoke to His people through the ministry of the prophets. After the Church was established, prophets continued to minister. The ministry of prophets did not cease after the deaths of the first century apostles and prophets.

Some scholars have promoted the idea that since we have scripture, there is no need for prophetic ministry. Others believe that since the Holy Spirit is in all believers, prophetic ministry is useless.

However, we should know that these doctrines are incorrect. Prophets and prophetic ministry are essential to God's purpose for the Church. God established this ministry in the Church second only to apostolic ministry.

The word prophet originates from the Greek word, prophetes, which means an inspired speaker or a foreteller. Prophets will only speak for God, not for a particular Church or organization.

Prophets are chosen to communicate the heart and mind of God. They are specialists in "the word of the Lord." Prophets' ministries will vary in demonstration and expression.

*Surely, the Lord God will do nothing, but he revealeth his secret unto his servants the prophets. (Amos 3:7)*

From the above verse and numerous examples in scripture, we know that prophets have a unique place in the kingdom of God.

## Prophets in the Old Testament

Before and after the establishment of the Mosaic Law and Old Covenant, prophets were used by God. The scriptures tell us of the prophetic ministry of Enoch. Abel, Adam's son, listed among those who are considered prophets.

*That the blood of all the PROPHETS, which was shed from the foundation of the world, may be required of this generation; From the blood of Abel unto the blood of Zacharias, which perished between the altar and the temple: verily I say unto you, It shall be required of this generation. (Luke11:50-51, Emphasis Mine)*

*And Enoch also, the seventh from Adam, prophesied of these, saying, Behold, the Lord cometh with ten thousands of his saints. (Jude 1:14)*

Aside from these, there are others, before the Law, who were prophets. One well-known prophet is Abraham. While rebuking Abimelech, God calls him a prophet.

*Now therefore restore the man his wife; for he is a prophet, and he shall pray for thee, and thou shalt live: and if thou restore her not, know thou that thou shalt surely die, thou, and all that are thine. (Genesis 20:7)*

Abraham's prophetic status was evident because of how the Lord used him. Abraham was used to represent the voice of the Lord in the earth. In addition, God revealed to him future events in his life and others (Sodom/Gomorrah and his descendants), as well as His eternal purpose. Even Christ said that Abraham saw His day before He came.

*Your father Abraham rejoiced to see my day: and he saw it and was glad. (John 8:56)*

Aside from Abraham, we see the greatest expression of the prophetic ministry after the institution of the Law. God used Moses, a prophet, to reveal His will for man's service to Him. After these things, God sent the prophets to Israel to cause them to return to Him and walk in His ways.

*Since the day that your fathers came forth out of the land of Egypt unto this day, I have even sent unto you all my servants the prophets, daily rising up early and sending them. (Jeremiah 7:25)*

In the Old Testament, the prophets came to perform certain tasks. God used the prophets to represent His voice to Israel and the surrounding nations. In the writings of Jeremiah, Ezekiel, and others, we see prophetic revelation concerning the nations. Also, God used the prophets to reveal God's plans for Israel and Judah even after He disciplined them.

> *I have also spoken by the prophets, and I have multiplied visions, and used similitudes, by the ministry of the prophets. (Hosea 12:10)*

The prophets had the task of challenging the sins of the people, calling them back into fellowship with God. The prophets were also excellent interpreters of the Law through divine inspiration. Through their ministries, they would correct erroneous doctrines surrounding the Law.

> *And thou shalt say unto them, Thus saith the Lord; If ye will not hearken to me, to walk in my law, which I have set before you, to hearken to the words of my*

*servants the prophets, whom I sent unto you, both rising up early, and sending them, but ye have not hearkened. (Jeremiah 26:4-5)*

The prophets of the Old Testament cried out against false prophets; revealing wolves in sheep's clothing.

*Then the Lord said unto me, The prophets prophesy lies in my name: I sent them not, neither have I commanded them, neither spake unto them: they prophesy unto you a false vision and divination, and a thing of nought, and the deceit of their heart. (Jeremiah 14:14)*

*Son of man, prophesy against the prophets of Israel that prophesy, and say thou unto them that prophesy out of their own hearts, Hear ye the word of the Lord;*

*Thus saith the Lord God; Woe unto the foolish prophets, that follow their own spirit, and have seen nothing! O Israel, thy prophets are like the foxes in the deserts. Ye have not gone up into the gaps, neither made up the hedge for the house of Israel to stand in the battle in the day of the Lord. They have seen vanity and lying divination, saying, The Lord saith: and the Lord hath not sent them: and they have made others to hope that they would confirm the word. (Ezekiel 13:2-6)*

In addition to the above tasks, the prophets revealed God's plan for individual as well as God's eternal purpose. Consider Jeremiah's words. He revealed God's purpose of redemption and salvation for Israel as a nation.

The prophets of old were not only men of rebuke and correction, but also men of vision and insight into God's good will for His people. Much of the recorded prophetic ministry came at a time when Israel and Judah were rebellious. However, the scriptures reveal that God had more to say to them than just repent. He wanted them to know His eternal plan and purpose for them as a nation.

> *Behold, the days come, saith the Lord, that I will make a new covenant with the house of Israel, and with the house of Judah. (Jeremiah 31:31)*

Therefore, we see that prophets have been around from the beginning. They have always been a part of God's working in the earth. With the establishment of the New Covenant and the Church, this did not change.

## Prophets in the New Testament

After the establishment of the Church, God

still used prophets. New Testament prophets fulfill the same functions as their Old Testament counterparts. They represent the voice of the Lord to the Church and world (however, this is done alongside other believers and ministers).

They are to be preachers of the Gospel of Jesus Christ. They challenge believers in their walks with the Lord. They call the Church to change and repentance and reveal future events.

In addition to the above functions, the New Testament prophet serves as a foundational ministry to the Church. On the day of Pentecost, God established His will for man's worship.

He no longer wanted to be "confined" to a building (represented by God's command to worship at the Temple), but dwell in the hearts of man. His will was for the believer to be His temple. As He abides in each individual, they corporately become the temple of God. Peter called the believers "stones" who are built together to form a spiritual house or temple where God could dwell.

> *Ye also, as lively stones, are built up a spiritual house, an holy priesthood, to offer up spiritual sacrifices, acceptable to God by Jesus Christ. (I Peter 2:5)*

> *What? Know ye not that your body is the temple of the Holy Ghost, which is in you, which ye have of God, and ye are not your own? (I Corinthians 6:19)*

With the New Covenant, the temple of God is now the hearts and minds of people. Their actual bodies become the habitation of God. Therefore, if the Church consists of people joined together by the presence of the Holy Spirit, then the foundation for the Church would consist of people also.

As Paul wrote to the believers, he revealed to them a very important truth. He told them that they (the Church) were built upon the foundation of the apostles and prophets with Christ being the head stone.

> *Now therefore ye are no more strangers and foreigners, but fellowcitizens with the saints, and of the household of God; And are built upon the foundation of the apostles and prophets, Jesus Christ himself being the chief corner stone; In whom all the building fitly framed together groweth unto an holy temple in the Lord: In whom ye also are builded together for an habitation of God through the Spirit. (Ephesians 2:19-22).*

In the above scripture, we discover certain truths. Paul was writing to a primarily Gentile audience. However, we must understand that the foundation that they stood upon was the same as the Jewish believers. Jewish and Gentile believers, alike, operated in the foundation established by the New Testament apostles and prophets.

The Church, like the New Covenant, was founded upon people, namely, the apostles and prophets. From this, we understand that since we will reign with Christ, God allowed man to have an active role in the establishment of the Church.

The apostles and prophets bear the responsibility for the Church, especially in doctrinal purity and spiritual direction. As Christ formed the foundation for the New Covenant, the apostles and prophets formed the foundation for the Church. Their ministries are foundational and continue to be major influences upon the Body of Christ.

The ministries of the apostles and prophets were needed to establish the Church, and their ministries are needed presently for the furtherance of the Church. Christ's ministry toward us is everlasting.

> *But this man, because he continueth ever, hath an unchangeable priesthood. Wherefore he is able also to save them to the uttermost that come unto God by him, seeing he ever liveth to make intercession for them. (Hebrews 7:24-25)*

The Book of Acts reveals to us the presence of prophets in the New Testament Church. Consider the following:

> *And in these days came prophets from Jerusalem unto Antioch. And there stood up one of them named Agabus and signified by the spirit that there should be great dearth*

*throughout all the world: which came to*
*pass in the days of Claudius Caesar. (Acts*
*11:27-28)*

The early Church benefited from the ministry of the prophets. We discover that the prophets traveled together.

A prophet of note among them was named Agabus. Through his ministry, the saints were prepared for a drought that came. They responded in sending help to the brethren that would be affected. Agabus also prepared Paul for the trials that awaited him in Jerusalem through prophetic insight.

*And as we tarried there many days, there*
*came down from Judaea a certain*
*prophet, named Agabus. And when he*
*was come unto us, he took Paul's girdle,*
*and bound his own hands and feet,*

*and said, Thus saith the Holy Ghost, So shall the Jews at Jerusalem bind the man that owneth this girdle, and shall deliver him into the hands of the Gentiles. (Acts 21:10-11)*

Aside from the foretelling of future events, we also discover that the New Testament prophet would strengthen and encourage the brethren through his ministry.

*And Judas and Silas, being prophets also themselves, exhorted the brethren with many words, and confirmed them. (Acts 15:32)*

Judas and Silas were recognized prophets in the early Church. They accompanied Paul and Barnabas back to Antioch with the elders' response to the requirements of Gentile believers. The above verse demonstrates to us that the prophet's ministry came to push the believers forward and establish them in the things of the Lord. In addition, we discover that when Silas joined Paul on his missionary journey that great ministry followed.

Not only did the New Testament prophets reveal future events and encourage the brethren, but also, they helped to launch ministries through prophetic insight.

*Now there were in the church that was at Antioch certain prophets and teachers; as Barnabas, and Simeon that was called Niger, and Lucius of Cyrene, and Manaen, which had been brought up with Herod the tetrarch, and Saul. As they ministered to the Lord, and fasted, the Holy Ghost said, Separate me Barnabas and Saul for the work whereunto I have called them. (Acts 13:1-2)*

In the Antioch church, it is apparent that prophets and teachers exercised the oversight. We find that as they ministered unto the Lord, the Lord spoke (it is likely through one of the prophets) to release Saul and Barnabas into the apostolic ministry. Saul (Paul) and Barnabas were recognized among the prophets and teachers.

However, through prophetic ministry, they were called forward to operate in another ministry. The New Testament prophet will do this occasionally. Along with the ministry of the prophets, the Book of Acts introduces us to individuals who had prophetic ministries and the gift of prophecy.

After Saul's (Paul's) conversion, the Lord spoke to a certain disciple named Ananias in a vision.

*And there was a certain disciple at Damascus, named Ananias; and to him said the Lord in a vision, Ananias. And he said, Behold, I am here, Lord. And the Lord said unto him, Arise, and go into the street which is called Straight, and inquire in the house of Judas for one called Saul, of Tarsus: for, behold, he prayeth, And hath seen in a vision a man named Ananias coming in, and putting his hand on him, that he might receive his sight. Then Ananias answered, Lord, I have heard by many of this man, how much evil he hath done to thy saints at Jerusalem: And here he hath authority from the chief priests to bind all that call on thy name. But the Lord said unto him, Go thy way: for he is a chosen vessel unto me, to bear my name before the Gentiles, and kings, and the children of Israel: For I will shew him how great things he must suffer for my name's sake. (Acts 9:10-16)*

The scriptures do not identify Ananias as a prophet, but a disciple. However, the depth of revelation and power that he operated in shows us that he walked in a prophetic anointing. God spoke to him personally. God's interaction with him is similar to how the Lord would speak to prophets.

When we consider other notable figures such as Peter (an apostle) and Philip (an evangelist and one of the seven), it is evident that these men possessed a prophetic anointing, though they were not prophets.

The scriptures not only reveal to us individuals who were prophets and had a prophetic anointing, but also those who had the gift of prophecy. Philip, the evangelist, had four daughters that had the gift of prophecy.

Some scholars want to identify them as prophetesses. However, the most popular translations of this passage in Acts only refer to them as having the gift of prophecy. They did not occupy the prophetic office.

*And the next day we that were of Paul's Paul's company departed and came unto Caesarea: and we entered into the house of Philip the evangelist, which was one of the seven; and abode with him. And the same man had four daughters, virgins, which did prophesy. (Acts 21:8-9 KJV)*

*And he had four maiden daughters who had the gift of prophecy. (Acts 21:9 Amplified)*

*He had four unmarried daughters who prophesied (Acts 21:9 NIV)*

From the above scriptures and references, we discover that the New Testament Church had prophets, individuals who possessed a prophetic anointing, and those who had the gift of prophecy. These gifts were needed then, and they are needed now.

There are theologians who twist the scriptures. In doing so, they assert that because we have the canon of scripture that prophets, prophetic ministry, and the gift of prophecy are no longer needed. The scriptures declare that Jesus Christ is the same yesterday, today, and forever (Hebrews 13:8). He ministered to the early Church through the prophets. He will not change until the end of all things.

If He used prophets and prophetic ministry in those times, He will continue to do so. Christ's ministry to the Church will not end until the

Judgment; therefore, the ministries of the prophets will not end until that Day

God is still using prophets today. In addition, God is raising up individuals who walk under and in a prophetic anointing that His glory may be seen in all.

# 2

# *The Call of a Prophet*

God calls men and women to the prophetic office in many ways. In the Old Testament, we discover that God called the prophets in different manners. However, we find that God's call to the prophetic office was a definite call.

The prophet's ministry is of importance to the Church and advancement of the Kingdom of God; therefore, God establishes them in their work through His calling.

There are individuals claiming to be prophets without having a significant call from the Lord. This chapter is designed to help believers recognize the prophetic calling upon others and themselves.  We will look at scriptural examples of how the Lord  called  individuals to understand the call of the prophet.

## Receiving the Prophetic Call

Prophets receive their callings in different manners. The most common ways are through dreams and visions, the voice of the Lord, and through others. Though the Lord can call someone to service in any way He chooses, these are most common.

### Ezekiel's Prophetic Call: Vision

Ezekiel received his prophetic call by way of vision. This is common among those called to the prophetic office.

**_Now it came to pass in the thirtieth year, in the fourth month, in the fifth day of the_**

*month, as I was among the captives by the*
*river of Chebar, that the heavens were*
*opened, and I saw visions of God. (Ezekiel*
*1:1)*

While by the river Chebar, Ezekiel had an open vision of the Lord. In this vision, the Lord commissioned him to his prophetic work. Though the vision contained various prophetic images, his call was clear. There are some individuals that claim that God gave them a dream or vision, but no definite call to ministry was evident.

*Jeremiah's Prophetic Call: The Voice of the Lord*

Jeremiah received his calling through the voice of the Lord. Every prophetic call may not be dramatic or involve others, but God will be clear as He reveals His plan.

**Then the word of the Lord came unto me,**

*saying, before I formed thee in the belly, I knew thee; and before thou camest forth out of the womb I sanctified thee, and I ordained thee a prophet unto the nations. (Jeremiah 1:4-5)*

When God's voice speaks to an individual concerning the prophetic office, there will be no denying it is from the Lord. When God spoke to Jeremiah, it was clear and understandable. The words he heard were not a product of his reasoning and thought. There are some who believe God spoke to them personally concerning their prophetic ministry, but they have no commission or charge with it. This is a sign that a person is only hearing his own thoughts.

*Elisha's Prophetic Call: Through Others*

Elisha's call to the prophet's office did not come through a dream or vision or directly from

God. The Lord spoke to Elijah to reveal Elisha's call to prophetic ministry.

> *And the Lord said unto him, Go, return on thy way to the wilderness of Damascus: and when thou comest, anoint Hazael to be king over Syria: And Jehu the son of Nimshi shalt thou anoint to be king over Israel: and Elisha the son of Shaphat of Abelmeholah shalt thou anoint to be prophet in thy room. (I Kings 19:15-16)*

> *So, he departed thence, and found Elisha the son of Shaphat, who was plowing with twelve yoke of oxen before him, and he with the twelfth: and Elijah passed by him, and cast his mantle upon him. (I Kings 19:19)*

The scriptures give no record of God speaking to Elisha, but when Elijah came, he knew what it meant to have the mantle placed upon him.

There are some individuals that God reveals the prophetic call through others. However, when this happens, a prophetic mantle (anointing) will be seen as a result of the revelation. There are some who received words of a call to the prophetic office but have never demonstrated any significant prophetic gifting and insight. There is a need for discernment in this area.

## Responding to the Prophetic Call

Continuing our examination of the call of the prophet leads us to an important aspect of the call. Once the calling is received, there must be a response from the prophet.

### Forsake Family

After Elijah placed his mantle upon him, Elisha knew it was an end to an era in his life. He understood that his call to the prophetic meant that a separation would come between him and his family.

> **And he left the oxen, and ran after Elijah, and said, Let me, I pray thee, kiss my father and my mother, and then I will follow thee. And he said unto him, Go back again: for what have I done to thee? (I Kings 19:20)**

When one receives the prophetic calling, there must be a forsaking of negative family and familial influences in his life. This is to ensure that the prophet will follow the word of the Lord and not deter from his task because of relationships.

## Forsake Self

During his commission to the prophetic office, God commanded Ezekiel not to be rebellious. Ezekiel was to minister to a rebellious people, but he was not to shun his ministry because of this.

> *But thou, son of man, hear what I say unto thee; Be not thou rebellious like that rebellious house: open thy mouth, and eat that I give thee. (Ezekiel 2:8)*

The prophetic ministry will bring the prophet into rejection, abuse, and ridicule. If the prophet is not selfless, he will disobey God in order to be accepted among the people. Though the New Testament prophet ministers to a redeemed people, they will meet opposition from carnal and immature saints.

*Forsake Fear*

Throughout Israel's history, the prophets were consistently persecuted. At the reception of his calling, Jeremiah was warned by the Lord not to be afraid. Though opposition was going to come, he was not to fear.

> *Thou therefore gird up thy loins, and arise, and speak unto them all that I command thee: be not dismayed at their faces, lest I confound thee before them. (Jeremiah 1:17)*

The call to the prophetic challenges the prophet to overcome internal and external fears. The prophet is to forsake fear of people and fear of failure. Some struggle with their call to the prophetic office because they are afraid that they will fail. But, if God places a calling on an individual's life, He will help them to fulfill it.

> *Being confident of this very thing, that he which hath begun a good work in you will perform it until the day of Jesus Christ: (Philippians 1:6)*

*Forsake Sin*

Isaiah saw the glory of the Lord when God called him into a greater prophetic work. Before he accepted his task, he had to recognize his own sinfulness and forsake it.

> ***Then said I, Woe is me! for I am undone; because I am a man of unclean lips, and I dwell in the midst of a people of unclean lips: for mine eyes have seen the King, the Lord of hosts. Then flew one of the seraphims unto me, having a live coal in his hand, which he had taken with the tongs from off the altar: And he laid it upon my mouth, and said, Lo, this hath touched thy lips; and thine iniquity is taken away, and thy sin purged. (Isaiah 6:5-7)***

Before the New Testament prophet can operate

fully in his calling, he has to be able to recognize his areas of sin and weakness. In addition, be willing to allow the Lord to bring him into a place of forsaking them. This will ensure longevity and purity in his ministry.

## Recognizing the Prophetic Call

Aside from clear and direct revelation from the Lord, there is no sure way to identify one who is called to the prophet's office. However, there are certain signs that may give indication of a prophetic call on an individual's life.

### *Revelatory Gifts*

One sign of a call to the prophet's office is the presence of the gifts of revelation in a believer's life. Individuals who consistently manifest the word of wisdom, word of knowledge, and discerning of spirits in their lives are likely candidates to stand in the prophet's office.

Usually a consistent manifestation of these gifts points toward individuals who possess a prophetic anointing, not towards those who are prophets.

*Consistent Visions & Dreams*

Individuals who consistently have visions and dreams may be budding prophets. Prophets are seers who consistently "see" into the Spirit.

> *And he said, Hear now my words: If there be a prophet among you, I the Lord will make myself known unto him in a vision, and will speak unto him in a dream. (Numbers 12:6)*

However, we must also remember that a by-product of the Spirit's outpouring is the increase in dreams and visions (Acts 2:17). In the New Testament Church, there will be an abundance of dreams and visions given to believers who are not prophets.

*Powerful Intercession*

Members of the Body of Christ who are intercessors may be upcoming prophets. One of the hallmarks of the prophet's ministry is intercession. They pray earnestly for the Church and its leaders

> **But if they be prophets, and if the word of the Lord be with them, let them now make intercession to the Lord of hosts...** **(Jeremiah 27:18)**

Conversely, we know that Jesus challenges all believers to be consistent in prayer. In addition, the apostles continually admonished the believers to be intercessors for one another. Again, intercession may be a sign of the prophetic office, not the manifestation of it.

*Prophetic Gifts*

One of the sure signs of a prophetic call is the presence of prophetic gifts such as the gift of prophecy and the gift of interpretation of tongues. The consistent manifestation of these gifts indicates that one may be called to the prophetic office.

> **The lion hath roared, who will not fear? the Lord God hath spoken, who can but prophesy? (Amos 3:8)**

The revelation of the Spirit is available to all believers. The prophetic gifts are consistent throughout the Body of Christ. Therefore, there is a company of believers who prophesy, without being prophets.

We must remember that the presence of prophetic gifts only serves as a sign of a call to the prophetic office. We have already stated that aside from clear and direct revelation from the Lord, there is no sure way to identify one who is called to the prophet's office. The above signs are only indications of a prophetic call.

Once a prophetic call is established, then the prophet goes through a process. In the next chapter, we will discuss the making of the prophet. Receiving the prophetic call is only the beginning; the next step is then preparation for walking in the prophetic office.

# 3

# *The Making of a Prophet*

The prophet's ministry comes with responsibility, authority, and power. In order for an individual to operate effectively in this ministry, his/her character has to be solid. Therefore, God will take the prophet through tests, trials, and temptations in order to prepare them for ministry.

The training of a prophet is sometimes painful. God will deal with every area in his life to prepare him for service. Those called to the prophetic office should understand that preparation for ministry is in character, not solely in the development of spiritual gifts.

In this chapter, we will discuss how God builds the

prophet for ministry.

## Crushing of the Prophet: The Potter's Wheel

Jeremiah prophesied to Judah during a time of great rebellion and sin against God. Prophetically, the Lord compared his dealing with Judah to a potter working on a wheel.

> *The word which came to Jeremiah from the Lord, saying, Arise, and go down to the potter's house, and there I will cause thee to hear my words. Then I went down to the potter's house, and, behold, he wrought a work on the wheels. And the vessel that he made of clay was marred in the hand of the potter: so he made it again another vessel, as seemed good to the potter to make it. (Jeremiah 18:1-4)*

Jeremiah saw the potter making a vessel that

seemed good in his eyes. God does this with the prophet. The prophet cannot decide what 'type' of prophet he will be. This is God's decision alone. His whole life becomes a prophetic example to the world.

Therefore, God will allow trials and sufferings as a part of the prophet's training and discipline. These are designed to produce humility in the prophet. God will build the prophet up only to break him down again so that the prophet knows that he is God's vessel and no longer his own.

In Jeremiah's description of the potter, it was the potter who marred the vessel. Most prophets have stories of great affliction and pain. It seems that God will allow them to be forsaken, ostracized, misunderstood, experience health problems, and the like in order to break down the mentality of the prophet. This is so God can build the prophet again into a vessel that will serve in holiness, power, and integrity.

Jeremiah saw the potter working on a solitary vessel. This implies that prophets will go through times of separation from their peers and other personalities as God makes them. God calls prophets to a greater level of self-death than others, so that His mind and heart will be communicated without personal biases or influences from the prophet.

In addition, God's training and crushing of the prophet continues throughout the life of the prophet to preserve him from personal sin and rebellion; that the word of the Lord from him will remain pure and untainted.

## Reverence of the Prophet: Isaiah's Vision

Isaiah's call to a greater prophetic ministry

was inaugurated with the reception of a vision of the Lord. While in the Temple, God revealed His glory to him. Isaiah saw the Lord upon His throne and His glory filling the Temple. He beheld the seraphim who cried out because of the Lord's holiness. Upon seeing these things, Isaiah realized God's greatness and his own sinfulness.

> *Then said I, Woe is me! for I am undone; because I am a man of unclean lips, and I dwell in the midst of a people of unclean lips: for mine eyes have seen the King, the Lord of hosts. (Isaiah 6:5)*

When God prepares the prophet for service, the prophet will be confronted with God's greatness. This is to produce in the prophet an unwavering reverence and fear for the Lord. In turn, the prophet will execute his ministry understanding the greatness of the One whom he represents.

Prophets will minister powerful messages from the Lord. Except the prophet respects God and understands his relationship to the Lord, the prophet will exalt his ministry above the God that called him.

When Isaiah saw God's glory, he realized his own sinfulness and that he could not glory in himself. The prophet today will experience a similar encounter with the Lord. Without a proper reverence for the Lord, the prophet may become disobedient or mishandle the prophetic ministry.

Thus, God will reveal His glory so that the prophet may fear. Prophetic ministry produces fear and respect for the prophet. However, the prophet has to understand that God will not share His glory.

*I am the Lord: that is my name: and my glory will I not give to another, neither my praise to graven images. (Isaiah 42:8)*

God reveals His glory so that the prophet will challenge the Body of Christ to reverence God. God uses men and women, but they are not to be equated with God, or be feared as God. God repeatedly declares His supremacy over men in the scriptures.

When God's process of developing reverence in the prophet is complete, the prophet will endeavor to turn the people's attention to God and not themselves as they minister.

## Building of the Prophet: Nebuchadnezzar's Dream

God develops humility and reverence in the prophet to build them into profitable servants. There are general characteristics that every prophet possesses as a result of the Lord's building process. The image that Nebuchadnezzar saw gives a clear illustration of how God builds the prophet. This image's head was of fine gold, his breast and his arms of silver, his belly and his thighs of brass, His legs of iron, his feet part of iron and part of clay.

> *Thou sawest till that a stone was cut out without hands, which smote the image upon his feet that were of iron and clay and brake them to pieces. (Daniel 2:32-34)*

*Head of Gold*

The head of gold reflects the wisdom, knowledge, understanding, and revelation that God gives the prophet. As gold is tried in the fire, so God will instruct, rebuke, and discipline the prophet in knowledge of His ways, statutes, and Word.

> *For thou preventest him with the blessings of goodness: thou settest a crown of pure gold on his head. (Psalms 21:3)*

*Breast and Arms of Silver*

The breast and arms of silver reflects the prophet's motivation for ministry. The breast (chest) is the place where the heart is, and the arms represent what the prophet will reach and strive for. Thus, as silver is purified, God builds the prophet to have proper motives in ministry.

**For thou, O God, hast proved us: thou hast tried us, as silver is tried. (Psalm 66:10)**

*Belly and Thighs of Brass*

The belly and thighs of brass reflects the prophet's resolve and stamina in ministry. The prophet has to have his fleshly desires under control (represented by the stomach) and walk upright before the Lord (represented by the thighs). The prophet is built to endure test and attacks, remaining faithful to the Lord and ministry.

> *Therefore, my beloved brethren, be ye stedfast, unmoveable, always abounding in the work of the Lord, forasmuch as ye know that your labour is not in vain in the Lord. (I Corinthians 15:58)*

## Feet of Iron and Clay

The feet of iron and clay reflect the prophet's authority in ministry. The iron represents the strength and authority of the Word that he will carry. The clay speaks of the prophet's humility while operating in great authority. The prophet must possess authority and humility as he performs his ministry.

> *For thou hast made him a little lower than the angels, and hast crowned him with glory and honour. Thou madest him to have*

*dominion over the works of thy hands; thou hast put all things under his feet. (Psalms 8:5-6)*

*Stone Made Without Hands*

At the end of the dream, a stone came and brake the image in pieces. We know that the stone was a representation of Christ. This reflects the prophet's submission to Christ in ministry. No matter how great God makes a prophet, he has to remember that if he exalts himself, God will bring him down.

*And whosoever shall exalt himself shall be abased; and he that shall humble himself shall be exalted. (Matthew 23:12)*

The greatness that a prophet has comes from God. The prophet has to walk in the knowledge that before Christ, his gifts, calling, and ministry mean nothing.

*Whosoever shall fall upon that stone shall be broken; but on whomsoever it shall fall, it will grind him to powder. (Luke 20:18)*

God crushes, produces reverence, and builds the prophet so that the prophet will have character conducive to facilitating pure and powerful prophetic ministry.

## The Prophet's Character: The Way of Love

Prophets speak for God, who is love. Regardless of the message delivered, the prophet's motivation for ministry has to be love. Love should be the foundation for the prophet's character. Love brings balance to the prophets as they deliver messages of rebuke and correction.

I Corinthians 13 gives us a list of the attributes of love. Fifteen traits are listed. Wherever the word "love" is, replace it with "a prophet." If prophets speak the heart of God, the heart of God must be in them.

> *Love is patient; love is kind. It does not envy; it does not boast; it is not proud. It is not rude; it is not self-seeking; it is not easily angered; it keeps no record of wrongs. Love does not delight in evil but rejoices with the truth. It always protects, always trusts, always hopes, always perseveres. Love never fails. (I Corinthians 13:4-8a NASV)*

*Patient.* Prophets have to be patient. Patience has to govern them as they wait to see the Church act on what God reveals to them. The prophet has the responsibility to deliver the word. The hearer has the task of carrying it out.

Prophets have to be patient with pastors and others as they follow the word spoken by them. The prophet may not know the timing that God has for a particular word.

> *And the servant of the Lord must not strive; but be gentle unto all men, apt to teach, patient. (II Timothy 2:24)*

*Kind.* Prophets have to be nice people. Because they sometimes will speak rebuke and correction, it is no excuse for them to be overbearing and rude. They have to behave as recipients of the grace and compassion of God.

*Not envious.* Prophets must resist the desire to compete. They should not be envious of another's ministry or position. Envy opens up the prophet to demonic influence in his life. James states that envy leads to evil.

*For where envying and strife is, there is confusion and every evil work. (James 3:16)*

Envying causes prophets to covet power and position. They will, in turn, prophesy from their own opinions and thoughts. This enables a stronghold of the enemy in their lives.

*Not boastful.* Prophets hear from God frequently. They have to guard themselves against bragging about their relationship with God.

God's call to ministry is a call to humility. Prophets must not use their gifts as a vehicle for promotion or honor. The true road to honor comes from obedience and submission to God.

*Humble yourselves in the sight of the Lord, and he shall lift you up. (James 4:10)*

*Not proud.* Prophets must resist pride at all costs.

God gives them great authority in the Spirit realm. However, they should not confuse their spiritual authority with self-worth. The call to ministry is not a platform for self-exaltation.

*But he giveth more grace. Wherefore he saith, God resisteth the proud, but giveth grace unto the humble. (James 4:6)*

Any prophet who operates in pride will not have a fruitful ministry. God's dealing with him will be infrequent and miniscule. Prophets should remember that God resists the proud.

*Not rude.* Prophets have to be courteous in their actions. Ministry is not an excuse for rude behavior. Some prophets blame their harsh statements and gestures on the Spirit. Though rebuke and correction do not feel or sound nice, it must be delivered out of a pure spirit.

Because prophets face rejection regularly, some are vulnerable to expressing their bitterness and hurt through ministry. Prophets are to avoid this at all costs.

*Not self-seeking.* Prophets must not regard or use their ministries as platforms for personal gain. They prophesy out of obedience to God, not man. Any self-seeking prophet walks in the way of Balaam, the false prophet, whom Balak asked to curse Israel.

Prophets that are self-seeking will become false prophets and share the same fate as he did. God rebuked him and later killed him.

*Which have forsaken the right way, and are gone astray, following the way of Balaam the son of Bosor, who loved the wages of unrighteousness; But was rebuked for his iniquity: the dumb ass speaking with man's voice forbad the madness of the prophet. (II 2:15-16)*

*Not easily angered.* Prophets become vulnerable to anger when they are ignored. Prophets have to remember, they represent God. If people do not listen to them, it is not grounds for them to become angry. Prophets speak for God and not themselves.

**For the wrath of man worketh not the righteousness of God. (James 1:20)**

Though prophets speak with the mind and wisdom of God, their anger does not always reflect this. Prophets who have tempers should remember the examples of Moses and Jonah. Moses, for his outburst of anger, was not allowed to enter into Canaan; while, Jonah endured a harsh lesson from the Lord.

*Keeps no record of wrong.* In personal and ministerial life, the prophet has to learn to forgive.

Forgiveness is the duty of all believers. Prophets have to be forgiving when they are misunderstood.

> *And be ye kind one to another, tenderhearted, forgiving one another, even as God for Christ's sake hath forgiven you. (Ephesians 4:32)*

Prophets, also, have to release individuals whom God forgives. Prophets see the sins and faults of others. They must learn to release individuals from past sins and not judge. In addition, prophets are not to share revealed sins to other believers.

*Does not rejoice in evil.* Prophets have to guard their hearts against being happy when individuals experience the discipline of God. Jonah hoped for the destruction of Nineveh; he was angered when God had mercy. Prophets have to remember that God's discipline comes because of His love. In addition, prophets must remember that God delights in mercy.

> **But go ye and learn what that meaneth, I will have mercy, and not sacrifice: for I am not come to call the righteous, but sinners to repentance. (Matthew 9:13)**

> **For he saith to Moses, I will have mercy on whom I will have mercy, and I will have compassion on whom I will have compassion. (Romans 9:15)**

*Rejoices with the truth.* Contrary to popular belief, prophets are not to be sad individuals. They should be able to rejoice with the truth, even in adverse settings.

> **For which cause we faint not; but though our outward man perish, yet the inward man is renewed day by day. (II Corinthians 4:16)**

Though some truth they carry may be unpopular, prophets have to learn to keep their spirits refreshed and renewed, even in persecution.

*Protects*. Prophets serve as protectors of the Word of God and the Church. Prophets will guard the Church against false doctrines and spiritual deception. In addition, they will help leadership protect immature and weak Christians. They will also aid in their restoration after a fall.

**We then that are strong ought to bear the infirmities of the weak, and not to please ourselves. (Romans 15:1)**

Always trusts. Prophets not only have to trust God, but also fellow believers. Prophets have to resist becoming judgmental of others, using "discernment" as an excuse. False discernment develops out of a bruised and hurt spirit. Prophets have to keep personal feelings aside in ministry. They need to learn to stay in the Spirit when discerning.

*Hopes*. Prophets are to live by faith and be able to inspire faith in others. Prophets are faced with adverse situations from the Church, family, and the enemy. Except hope remains, the prophet will become subject to disappointment and discouragement. This is what happened to Jeremiah. He asked,

> **Why is my pain perpetual, and my wound incurable, which refuseth to be healed? Wilt thou be altogether unto me as a liar, and as waters that fail? (Jeremiah 15:18)**

Jeremiah had lost hope because his ministry met great opposition. A true prophet's ministry is always under scrutiny and judgment. Without hope, the prophet will become burnt-out and disillusioned.

*Perseveres*. Prophets need endurance. They have to persevere through the tests of God, temptations of the devil, trials of men, and the troubles of life. Without perseverance, prophets will give up during hard times. In addition, their lives and ministries will be short-lived.

The gifts and callings of God are without repentance, but the nature of God has to be developed. Because of the spiritual depth of their ministries, prophets need depth of character for balance. Prophets will not fail in their ministries as long as they walk in love.

# 4

# *The Office of the Prophet*

We have discussed what a prophet is, the call of a prophet, and the making of a prophet. It is time now time to address the prophet's role in the Church. It has been stated that there is diversity in the demonstration and operation of prophetic gifts. However, prophets share in the execution of their ministries some common attributes. Though not all prophets are the same, there are certain characteristics that they possess. All prophets exhibit characteristics of messengers and interpreters.

## Prophets as Messengers

God calls prophets for one purpose. They

are to be His messengers. Messengers play important roles in society. Without them, communication may be hindered. The same is true in the Kingdom of God. Without prophets and prophetic ministry, the communication between God and man may be frustrated.

*Messengers are deliverers of the sender's message.* A messenger's only task is to carry the message from the sender to the recipient. God calls prophets to deliver the Word (message) of the Lord. Though they may function in other areas in ministry, this is their primary task.

> **But when I speak with thee, I will open thy mouth, and thou shalt say unto them, Thus saith the Lord God; He that heareth, let him hear; and he that forbeareth, let him forbear: for they are a rebellious house. (Ezekiel 3:27)**

*Messengers are responsible for the message they carry.* Messengers have to be careful not to lose or damage the message given them. Some messengers have to deliver oral messages as well as written. Prophets are responsible for the Word that God will give them.

> **So thou, O son of man, I have set thee a watchman unto the house of Israel; therefore, thou shalt hear the word at my mouth, and warn them from me. (Ezekiel 33:7)**

Prophets are the eyes of the Lord. They have to watch in the Spirit for what the Lord will say and deliver His message to the people. If they do not do this, they will not be successful in ministry and subject themselves to the discipline of God.

The scriptures call the prophets "watchmen" and not shepherds. Though God will reveal many things to them in the Spirit, they must minister those words in submission to local leadership.

*Messengers must not alter the message given.* Messengers have to be careful to deliver the given message only. The messenger has to be careful not to tamper with the message in any way. Likewise, prophets have to deliver the Word as God gives it to them.

> **The prophet that hath a dream, let him tell a dream; and he that hath my word, let him speak my word faithfully. What is the chaff to the wheat? saith the Lord. (Ezekiel 23:28)**

They should not alter the message because of personal opinion/bias, popularity, or gain. Prophets have to resist prophesying to earn the favor of men. In addition, they have to guard themselves against ministering to bring people under their control. Prophets that alter the word of the Lord are candidates for becoming false prophets.

*Messengers have to be fearless.* Messengers have been killed for the message they delivered. Throughout history, there are numerous stories of messengers who are killed for relaying another's message. Therefore, a messenger has to be fearless.

Prophets have to be bold in their ministries. There is no place for fear in the life of a prophet. Prophets must deliver the message that God gives in spite of the consequences. This is why when God called Jeremiah, He encouraged him to be fearless.

> **Be not afraid of their faces: for I am with thee to deliver thee, saith the Lord. (Jeremiah 1:8)**

Numerous prophets have ruined their ministries because they would not prophesy what the Lord said. They would change God's word into one of prosperity, healing, and deliverance without mentioning His discipline, correction, and rebuke.

*Messengers have to be trustworthy.* A messenger has to have the trust of the one who sends him. The messenger is the link between the sender and recipient. Thus, he has to be trusted in order to have such a responsibility. The Lord entrusts prophets with His Word.

> **Surely the Lord God will do nothing, but he revealeth his secret unto his servants the prophets. (Amos 3:7)**

Prophets are to possess integrity. God chooses to reveal His plans unto the prophets. God will always speak to His prophets as He prepares to move in the earth. Prophets must not take this lightly. They have to be faithful to their ministries.

## Prophets as Interpreters

Important to any kingdom are interpreters. Interpreters are there to help foreign nations understand the messages of sending governments and ambassadors. Prophets perform this role in the Kingdom of God.

Interpreters are important to any kingdom. Interpreters are a valuable resource to any kingdom. They provide nations with the opportunity to communicate with one another without confusion.

Prophets have always been an important part of the plan of God in the earth. In the Old Testament, God used prophets to reveal His counsel. In the Church, prophets play an important role in the revelation of Christ to the world.

*Interpreters understand more than one language.* Interpreters have the important task of establishing communication between people of different nationalities and languages. Prophets understand the various manners in which God speaks.

They help believers understand the different ways in which God speaks. They are skilled interpreters of dreams, visions, signs, and events.

> *I have also spoken by the prophets, and I have multiplied visions, and used similitudes, by the ministry of the prophets. (Hosea 12:10)*

Prophets have the awesome responsibility to make known unto man the counsel of an invisible God.

*Interpreters are skilled in communication.* Interpreters are more than translators. It is a known fact that it is possible to lose meaning through literal translation.

Therefore, it is imperative that the interpreter be able to not only translate, but also communicate the intent of the words spoken. Prophets have to be able to communicate the heart and mind of God as well as the Word of God.

*Interpreters do not work alone.* When an interpreter is present, he is not the primary communicator. The interpreter's function is secondary to those who are conversing, though vital. Prophets do not work alone. Oftentimes, they are seen in groups.

> ***And Saul sent messengers to take David: and when they saw the company of the prophets prophesying, and Samuel standing as appointed over them... (I Samuel 19:20a)***

Prophets also work aside other ministries to ensure that the counsel of God is understood. In addition, they labor to ensure its proper application in the Church and in the lives of believers.

## Nine Functions of the Prophet

Prophetic ministry is unique. Though there are differences in the administration and demonstration of prophetic gifts, all prophets have essentially the same functions within the Church.

*Preach/Teach the Word of God.* Contrary to popular belief, prophets not only speak under prophetic inspiration, but also expound on the Word of God. Prophets will preach and teach the Word with clarity.

The Old Testament prophets proved to be excellent interpreters of the Law; their New Testament counterpart did the same. They will explain hidden mysteries in the Word.

*Whereby, when ye read, ye may understand my knowledge in the mystery of Christ); which in other ages was not made known unto the sons of men, as it is now revealed unto his holy apostles and prophets by the Spirit. (Ephesians 3:4-5)*

*And Judas and Silas, being prophets also themselves, exhorted the brethren with many words, and confirmed them. (Acts 15:32)*

*Serve as Intercessors.* Prophets serve as powerful intercessors. They have an awesome burden to see the will of God. Prophets will pray for extended times and periods. Scholars call Jeremiah the "weeping prophet." This was due to his continual intercession for Israel.

*But if they be prophets, and if the word of the Lord be with them, let them now*

*make intercession to the Lord of hosts...*
*(Jeremiah 27:18a)*

*Lay Spiritual Foundations.* Prophets have the authority and anointing to lay spiritual foundations in the Church. Prophets are equipped to reveal hidden truths of God's Word and lay foundations for the people of God to grow thereby.

**And are built upon the foundation of the apostles and prophets, Jesus Christ himself being the chief corner stone. (Ephesians 2:20)**

*Reveal/Impart Spiritual Gifts (I Timothy 4:14).* Prophets have the ability to recognize the gifts of God in believers. They have the ability to impart wisdom, knowledge, and understanding. Prophets can bring to light spiritual gifts resident in believers and impart gifts (by the direction of the Spirit) through the laying on of hands.

*Now there were in the church that was at Antioch certain prophets and teachers; as Barnabas, and Simeon that was called Niger, and Lucius of Cyrene, and Manaen, which had been brought up with Herod the tetrarch, and Saul. As they ministered to the Lord, and fasted, the Holy Ghost said, Separate me Barnabas and Saul for the work whereunto I have called them. And when they had fasted and prayed, and laid their hands on them, they sent them away. (Acts 13:1-3)*

*Prophesy (Acts 11:27-28).* Prophets are divinely gifted to prophesy. Their prophecies will be of a greater depth and clarity than other believers who have the gift of prophecy. They will prophesy frequently and accurately.

They will have a consistent track record of prophetic words that are true. This is the foundation of their ministry. Though they will intercede, pray, and preach, prophesying is their first priority.

> *Moreover, he said unto me, Son of man, all my words that I shall speak unto thee receive in thine heart, and hear with thine ears. And go, get thee to them of the captivity, unto the children of thy people, and speak unto them, and tell them, Thus saith the Lord God; whether they will hear, or whether they will forbear. (Ezekiel 3:10-11)*

*Interpret Signs, Wonders, Dreams, and Visions.* Prophets are gifted to interpret the supernatural manifestations of God. Some are gifted like Daniel in understanding dreams and visions. Others will be able to interpret seemingly natural events through which God is speaking. In addition, prophets will see dreams and visions on a regular basis.

> *And he said, Hear now my words: If there*

*be a prophet among you, I the Lord will make myself known unto him in a vision, and will speak unto him in a dream. (Numbers 12:6)*

*Expose False Prophets and Doctrines.* Prophets are stewards of the mysteries of God. They have revelation and foresight to warn against spiritual deception. They will contend for purity of faith and doctrine in the Church. They, like prophets of old, will warn and speak against false prophets and ministers, unashamedly. Jeremiah, the prophet, cried out against the false leaders in his day.

*The prophets prophesy falsely, and the priests bear rule by their means; and my people love to have it so: and what will ye do in the end thereof? (Jeremiah 5:31)*

*Performs Signs, Wonders and Healings.* Prophets

will have signs and wonders in their ministry. The signs and wonders will manifest to confirm the spoken prophetic word. Isaiah prophesied to Hezekiah that God would heal him. God honored Isaiah's word by granting him a sign.

> *And this shall be a sign unto thee from the Lord, that the Lord will do this thing that he hath spoken; Behold, I will bring again the shadow of the degrees, which is gone down in the sun dial of Ahaz, ten degrees backward. So, the sun returned ten degrees, by which degrees it was gone down. (Isaiah 38:7-8)*

*Establish Believers, Churches, and Organizations in the Faith and Will of God.* Prophets have the chore to bring the people back to the purity of the faith. They have the ability to promote growth and stability in the Body of Christ.

In addition, through prophetic insight, they will endeavor to make sure that the plan and will of God is accomplished. Silas, a prophet, accompanied Paul in ministry. As a result, the churches were strengthened in the faith.

*And Paul chose Silas, and departed, being recommended by the brethren unto the grace of God. And he went through Syria and Cilicia, confirming the churches. (Acts 15:40-41)*

Focus of Prophets

Prophetic individuals operate the same as the brain in the human body. Prophets have the responsibility to communicate the mind and thoughts of God. They will have insight into what God is saying and doing. However, they must be careful not to misinterpret the mind of God based upon their emotions and biases.

Though prophets are keenly aware of the love of God, their words will mobilize people to action after the father-son relationship is established. Prophetic individuals will know how to articulate the Word of the Lord and inspire others to follow His commands. God created man for His glory and for fulfilling His purpose. The prophetic ministry is given to see this fulfilled in the earth.

# 5

# *The Prophetic Person*

Though God uses prophets, they are not the only individuals who are able to communicate the word of the Lord. Even in the Old Testament, we discover that God wanted His Spirit to dwell in mankind that they all could know His voice and express His counsel. Moses, through prophetic insight, made this point clear to Joshua.

> *And Moses said unto him, Enviest thou for my sake? Would God that all the Lord's people were prophets, and that the Lord would put his spirit upon them! (Numbers 11:29)*

Moses understood that God wanted all His people

to be able to speak for Him. With this in view, we find in the New Testament that God gives believers the gift of prophecy and the prophetic anointing to declare His counsel without occupying the office of the prophet. This is so the prophets will not have to do all the prophesying and that the counsel of God will reach all believers.

The individual who possesses a prophetic anointing upon his/her life is referred to as a prophetic person. Prophetic people possess the same characteristics as the prophets. They act as messengers and interpreters, though not with the same level of influence and authority.

## The Prophetic Person is a Messenger

Prophetic people are called for one purpose. They are in the Body of Christ to ensure that prophetic ministry is received and given in the proper manner.

Prophetic people have the responsibility to be messengers like the prophets. However, the scope and authority of their gifting is less than that of the prophet.

*Messengers are deliverers of the sender's message.* Prophetic people have the responsibility to speak the message of the Lord to others in the Body. They will do this while in subjection to the structure of the local assembly and under the supervision of leadership and mature prophetic ministers.

> **But when I speak with thee, I will open thy mouth, and thou shalt say unto them, Thus saith the Lord God; He that heareth, let him hear; and he that forbeareth, let him forbear: for they are a rebellious house. (Ezekiel 3:27)**

*Messengers are responsible for the message they carry.* Messengers must be careful not to lose or damage the message given them. Some messengers must deliver oral messages as well as written. Prophetic people are responsible for the Word that God will give them. Prophetic people have to be careful not to speak anything aside from what God gives them.

> *So thou, O son of man, I have set thee a watchman unto the house of Israel; therefore, thou shalt hear the word at my mouth, and warn them from me. (Ezekiel 33:7)*

*Messengers must not alter the message given.* Messengers must be careful to deliver the given message only. The messenger has to be careful not to tamper with the message in any way.

Likewise, prophetic people must deliver the Word as God gives it to them. They should not alter the message because of personal opinion/bias, popularity, or gain.

> **The prophet that hath a dream, let him tell a dream; and he that hath my word, let him speak my word faithfully. What is the chaff to the wheat? saith the Lord. (Jeremiah 23:28)**

*Messengers have to be fearless.* Messengers have been killed for the message they delivered. Throughout history, there are numerous stories of messengers who are killed for relaying another's message. Therefore, a messenger has to be fearless.

Prophetic people will be bold in declaring the revelation God gives them. They cannot fear rejection of man, but rather live to please God.

> **Be not afraid of their faces: for I am**

*with thee to deliver thee, saith the Lord. (Jeremiah 1:8)*

*Messengers have to be trustworthy.* A messenger must have the trust of the one who sends him. Prophetic people must have the trust of the Lord, leadership, and the brethren in order to be received properly. Prophetic people are to possess integrity. They have to be faithful to Christ and the Church.

## The Prophetic Person as an Interpreter

*Important to any kingdom are interpreters.* Interpreters are there to help foreign nations understand the messages of sending governments and ambassadors. Interpreters are a valuable resource. They provide nations with the opportunity to communicate with one another without confusion.

Prophetic people help other believers to understand the move and will of God. They help individuals to apply the Word delivered by leadership to their particular situations.

*Interpreters understand more than one language.* Interpreters have the important task of establishing communication between people of different nationalities and languages. Prophetic people, like prophets, will be gifted to understand the different ways that God speaks. Some are able to interpret dreams and visions. Others will be able to show how everyday events speak prophetically to individuals.

*Interpreters are skilled in communication.* Interpreters are more than translators. It is a known fact that it is possible to lose meaning through literal translation. Therefore, it is imperative that the interpreter be able to not only translate, but also communicate the intent of the words spoken. Prophetic people have to be able to communicate the heart and mind of God as well as His words.

*Interpreters do not work alone.* When an interpreter is present, he is not the primary communicator. Oftentimes, they work alongside ambassadors. The interpreter's function is secondary to those who are conversing, though vital.

Prophetic people do not work alone. They minister in connection with other mature members and leadership to ensure the counsel of God is understood. In addition, they endeavor to see its proper application in the Church and in believers' lives.

## The Prophetic Person's Character

Because prophetic people have the gifts of God consistently operating in their lives, their characters must be developed and be conducive to facilitating prophetic ministry. Without character, prophetic people will become deceived, prideful, and move in a realm that is reserved only for prophets.

Jesus' "Sermon on the Mount" began with what is called "The Beatitudes" (Matthew 5:3-12). These attitudes should be demonstrated in all believers. However, the prophetic person must use Jesus' words to govern their characters.

1) Blessed are the poor in spirit. Prophetic people have to be humble. Because God uses them to communicate His messages, humility will bring stability to them and protect them against deception.

2) Blessed are those who mourn. Prophetic people have to be broken before God. They should grieve over the sins of the Church and make intercession to God on behalf of the people.

3) Blessed are those who are meek. Prophetic people have to be mild-mannered and even-tempered. They cannot be governed by their emotions, nor bound by biases and anger. Though God may use them to challenge others, they have to do it in the proper spirit.

4) Blessed are those who hunger and thirst for righteousness. Prophetic people have to be holy. Their daily task is to reflect the holiness and righteousness of God in their walk with Him.

5) Blessed are those who are merciful. Prophetic people should be compassionate and forgiving. Compassion will help them to minister without condemnation, while forgiveness will keep their hearts pure toward others, even in light of persecution, rejection, and misunderstanding.

6) Blessed are the pure in heart. Prophetic people must have the right motives in ministering.

They do not minister for popularity or position, but because of the love of God and the brethren.

Again, if these do not govern prophetic people, they leave themselves open for a snare and trap of the devil.

## Identifying the Prophetic Person

Prophetic people are dispersed in the Body by the discretion of the Spirit. Some people who possess a prophetic anointing do not recognize it. To aid in the identification of the prophetic anointing, let us look at how prophetic people will function within the Body.

**Prophetic people proclaim the Word of God.** Prophetic people love the written Word of God. They know how to prophetically interpret scriptures. They boldly speak the Word. The written Word must live in them before they declare the prophetic word of the Lord.

> *Let the word of Christ dwell in you richly in all wisdom; teaching and admonishing one another in psalms and hymns and spiritual songs, singing with grace in your hearts to the Lord. (Colossians 3:16)*

**Prophetic people are intercessors.** Prophetic people are powerful intercessors. They are instant in prayer. They know how to intercede for the people of God according to His will. They have consistent prayer lives. They take the burdens of others upon themselves to present them to God.

> *Let every one of us please his neighbor for his good to edification. For even Christ pleased not himself; but, as it is written, The reproaches of them that reproached thee fell on me. (Romans 15:2-3)*

Prophetic people motivate believers to fulfill the will of God. Prophetic people have the ability to recognize gifts and ministries in others. They help others to recognize their gifts and use them according to the will of God while respecting established leadership.

**Prophetic people declare the prophetic word of the Lord.** Prophetic people have the gift of prophecy. Yet, their prophetic words will not have the same anointing, clarity, and depth of the prophet. Their words will edify, exhort, and comfort the Body of Christ.

> *But he that prophesieth speaketh unto men to edification, and exhortation, and comfort. He that speaketh in an unknown tongue edifieth himself; but he that prophesieth edifieth the church. (I Corinthians 14:3)*

**Prophetic people interpret dreams, visions, and signs.** Prophetic people have the ability to interpret dreams and visions. Some frequently have dreams, visions, and impressions. They are able to interpret the languages of God with success.

**Prophetic people expose false prophets and doctrines.** Prophetic people have the spiritual insight to recognize error. Through the revelation of the Spirit and by their knowledge of the Word, they warn others against deception and false ministry.

> *Beloved, believe not every spirit, but try the spirits whether they are of God: because many false prophets are gone out into the world. (I John 4:1)*

**Prophetic people have other gifts operating in them.** Along with the gift of prophecy, prophetic people have other gifts of the Spirit. Most common among them is the discerning of spirits, the interpretation of tongues, the word of knowledge, and the word of wisdom

> **But all these worketh that one and the selfsame Spirit, dividing to every man severally as he will. (I Corinthians 12:11)**

## Walking as a Prophetic Person

If you feel you have a prophetic anointing upon your life, it will not flourish if you are not consistent in your relationship with the Lord. The following steps are necessary to walk consistently in a prophetic anointing.

*Study the Word of God.* Prophetic people must consistently study and apply the Word of God to their lives. They must remember that every prophetic word spoken must be in line with the scriptures. If there is no knowledge of the Word, prophecies given are likely to be in error. The written Word will bring balance to the prophetic ministry.

> *We have also a more sure word of prophecy; whereunto ye do well that ye take heed, as unto a light that shineth in a dark place, until the day dawn, and the day star arise in your hearts. (II Peter 1:19)*

*Have an established prayer life.* Prophetic people have to be consistent in prayer. It is the only way to remain strong in the Lord. Prayer is the vehicle through which prophetic words are received. Praying keeps the prophetic anointing fresh. If you want to walk in the prophetic, an unwavering prayer life is mandatory.

> *Rejoice evermore. Pray without ceasing. In everything give thanks: for this is the will of God in Christ Jesus concerning you. (I Thessalonians 5:16-18)*

*Submit to Leadership.* Prophetic people have to be submitted to local leadership. They must follow the vision of the leaders as they follow Christ. Though they have prophetic insight, they are not to think they are more spiritual than leadership and other members.

In order for the prophetic ministry to remain in them, they must respect the authority that God has placed over them. They have to respect authority before God entrusts them with the authority to speak His word.

**For I am a man under authority...**
**(Matthew 8:9a)**

The centurion received a blessing from Christ because he respected His authority. Likewise, prophetic people will receive revelation from the Spirit as they respect God-given leadership.

# 6

# *Prophets in Perspective*

The increase of revelation and information opens the path to deception through excess. As we endeavor to learn more about God and His ministries, we must avoid extremes. History has shown that every time God has moved in the earth, the enemy has tried to counterattack with excess and deception. We see this trend today with the emerging prophetic ministries. In this chapter, we will endeavor to bring balance to the numerous teachings surrounding prophets. In short, we want to keep our outlook on the office in perspective.

## Prophets and the Church

In the first chapter, we stated that prophetic

ministry is a foundational ministry in the Church. Foundational does not mean that this ministry is more important or valuable than other ministries. When considering a building, the foundation is not seen. However, when storms and other influences come against the building, the foundation's strength provides support for the building.

The same is true for the Church. When prophets minister properly, they will not be the center of attention, but the entire Church will display the nature of Christ and the power of God.

The true purpose of prophets is that their ministries help the Church stand against attacks of the enemy and deception. However, we see that the Church has lost vision, purpose, and power. This is because true prophetic ministry is missing. Consequently, the Church promotes false doctrines and ministers unwittingly. In addition, it is divided over unimportant issues. The Church has left the simplicity of Christ to follow another gospel, based upon prosperity and not righteousness.

> *But I fear, lest by any means, as the serpent beguiled Eve through his subtilty, so your minds should be corrupted from the simplicity that is in Christ. For if he that cometh preacheth another Jesus, whom we have not preached, or if ye receive another spirit, which ye have not received, or another gospel, which ye have not accepted, ye might well bear with him. (II Corinthians 11:3-4)*

The error of many prophets is that they have drawn attention to themselves and their gifts and have neglected their responsibilities to the Church. As a result, the whole Church suffers. Prophets are to minister so that the Church may shine.

*For all things are for your sakes, that the abundant grace might through the thanksgiving of many redound to the glory of God. (II Corinthians 4:15)*

*Therefore, I endure all things for the elect's sakes, that they may also obtain the salvation which is in Christ Jesus with eternal glory. (II Timothy 2:10)*

Prophets are to have this mentality as they minister. They minister so the Church would remain partakers of the grace of God unto salvation. The foundation supports the building. When prophets fulfill their tasks, local assemblies, churches, and organizations are healthy and vibrant.

The problem remains that individuals in the Body of Christ are exalting apostles, prophets, and other ministers above measure in the Church. The Church has to be sober in its acceptance of prophets. They have to remember that prophets are men and women redeemed by Christ. Their gifts do not make them special or superior.

Their gifts and ministries make them responsible for the Church. Many prophets fall into pride and rebellion because men esteem them too highly. What, then, is to be the Church's approach to prophets?

> *For I say, through the grace given unto me, to every man that is among you, not to think of himself more highly than he ought to think; but to think soberly, according as God hath dealt to every man the measure of faith. For as we have many members in one body, and all members have not the same office: So we, being many, are one body in Christ, and every one members one of another. (Romans 12:3-5)*

Paul instructed the Romans that they were not to think too much of themselves. However, we must remember not to think too much of prophets. Why? He goes on to say that God has given every man a measure of faith to operate in whatever ministry or gift he has.

Therefore, since God is the source of all gifts, there is no need for the saints to think of anyone too highly. Yet, we are to give respect and honor unto one another as members of Christ.

*Render therefore to all their dues: tribute to whom tribute is due; custom to whom custom; fear to whom fear; honour to whom honour. (Romans 13:7)*

Paul told the Romans that they were to give respect unto the leaders in government. Whatever office they held, he told them to give them the respect the office demanded. The same applies to apostles, prophets, and other ministries. We are to respect them for their service in the Lord, especially those who labor for our spiritual well-being (this speaks very heavily to pastors).

*For if a man think himself to be something, when he is nothing, he deceiveth himself. But let every man prove his own work, and then shall he have rejoicing in himself alone, and not in another. (Galatians 6:3-4)*

Prophets are not to boast about their labors, for it leads to deception. Conversely, they are to rejoice before the Lord because of the reward He gives.

## Prophets and Pastors

The enemy is the author of confusion and division. If he can keep the leaders in the Church divided, they will not minister effectively in the Church. We have already addressed the fact that prophets are not to think more  highly of themselves than they ought. However, since pastors usually have the oversight of local churches and assemblies, there is a need for understanding between prophets and pastors.

At the heart of the strife and tension between prophets and pastors is the need for control blurred by personal insecurities. When a pastor has a prophet in his church, he must not allow insecurity and intimidation to grip his spirit. If so, he will perceive everything the prophet does as a challenge to his authority.

Conversely, the prophet should not try to handle situations reserved for the pastor of the Church. The pastor has the responsibility for the souls of the sheep. He also bears the responsibility for the spiritual oversight of the prophets that are in fellowship with the assembly.

Oftentimes, the enemy causes a war between pastors and prophets. The pastors feel intimidated by the manner in which God uses the prophets, and the prophets feel that the pastor is against them because of a persecution complex. The need for communication is vital.

Without communication, there will be confusion, and no one will benefit, but the kingdom of Satan. Pastors must resist fighting prophets to feel like they are in control. Control is not the issue, but ministry. However, prophets have to learn to be subject to leadership if they expect to have fruitful ministries.

All ministries are needed in the Body of Christ. Pastors cannot devalue the ministries of prophets because they are under their ministries. Pastors need to understand that this ministry is foundational and is an asset to any ministry.

Conversely, prophets cannot feel that they are "above" pastors because of the authority and anointing upon their lives. Ministries are given to work together in peace. It is with this understanding that prophets and pastors have to work together in the local church or assembly.

**Apostles versus Prophets**

Another reoccurring trend in the Body of Christ is apostles trying to function as prophets and prophets trying to function as apostles without the anointing or call of the Lord. Apostles will have to function sometimes in prophetic voices in the Body of Christ. However, this is not to be their area of concern. Their main job is to advance the Kingdom of God, not to be prophets.

Because some apostles have become deceived, thinking that they are all of the ministry gifts wrapped into one, they began to prophesy beyond the measure of their gifts. This turns into a soulish prophetic ministry, which usually ends up with the apostle thinking that he cannot ever be wrong.

The apostle begins to prophesy for money and personal gain. Then, the apostle usually develops a following based upon his personality rather than the person of Christ. The result is then a deceived apostle with a following of beguiled souls.

Prophets also must guard themselves against thinking that God is going to elevate them to the apostolic office. It is true that Paul was a prophet/teacher before entering apostolic ministry. However, this was at the call of the Lord. With some, God does use the prophetic office as training for the apostolic office.

Many prophets, though, have taken it upon themselves to try to operate as apostles. They begin to start ministries and churches claiming apostolic authority and right. The result is a deceived prophet whose prophetic ministry is stifled by deception.

Though there are similarities between apostles and prophets, they must resist intruding on one another's offices based upon their own desires. In addition, apostles and prophets have to resist competing among themselves as to which office takes preeminence in the Church.

The Word declares that He placed the apostles first. However, all ministries are equally important to the plan and purpose of God in the earth. No ministry is better, though functions differ. Apostles and prophets have to learn how to relate to one another through the Spirit, balanced by humility and love.

In order for the church to keep Prophets and Prophetic ministry in the proper perspective, misconceptions of this office must be addressed.

**Responding to Misconceptions**

There are many false beliefs circulating about prophets and their ministries. We shall now explore some of the prevailing misconceptions surrounding the prophetic office.

*I. Prophets are not to be subject to leadership*

Prophets are not to override leadership, though they possess great authority and revelation. If they are not the pastors or heads of the organization, they are not to function outside of the parameters established by the existing leaders.

The Old Testament prophets were always subject to the king, though they had to prophesy and cry out against certain activities. In the New

Testament church, we discover prophets were subject to leadership.

> **Then pleased it the apostles and elders, with the whole church, to send chosen men of their own company to Antioch with Paul and Barnabas; namely, Judas surnamed Barsabas, and Silas, chief men among the brethren. (Acts 15:22)**

After the letter was written to establish the Gentile believers in the faith, the apostles and elders sent Judas and Silas (who were both prophets) to deliver the message with Paul and others. They did not choose to go, but the apostles and elders sent them.

*II. Prophets are to be lone rangers*

Prophets are a part of the Body of Christ. The

prophets are to function within the community of believers. Some feel that prophets are to be by themselves. This is because they felt that the Old Testament prophets were loners. We understand by the Word that the prophets normally surfaced in groups and some held positions in the government.

> *And in these days came prophets from Jerusalem unto Antioch. And there stood up one of them named Agabus, and signified by the spirit that there should be great dearth throughout all the world: which came to pass in the days of Claudius Caesar. (Acts 11:27-28)*

*III. Revelation doesn't have to be clear.*

There are prophets who minister and the individual leaves their presence confused. The revelation of a mature prophet will be clear. Prophets declare the word of the Lord. How can the believer obey God if the word is confusing? Now, the prophecy should be clear, though the interpretation of it may not be. This is where prayer is vital.

Prayer after the word is given will lead to a proper interpretation. Paul stated that God was not the author of confusion after he spoke of the prophets and prophetic ministry in the local church.

> *If anything be revealed to another that sitteth by, let the first hold his peace. For ye may all prophesy one by one, that all may learn, and all may be comforted. And the spirits of the prophets are subject to the prophets. For God is not the author of confusion, but of peace, as in all churches of the saints. (I Corinthians 14:30-33)*

*IV. Prophets always have a word.*

Though God reveals many things to prophets, there are times when God will not give the prophets a word or authorize them to speak a word. Prophets are only prophets when inspired by God to speak. Even Elisha, who had a double portion of Elijah's spirit, did not have a word concerning the woman who came to him about her son.

> **And when she came to the man of God to the hill, she caught him by the feet: but Gehazi came near to thrust her away. And the man of God said, Let her alone; for her soul is vexed within her: and the Lord hath hid it from me, and hath not told me. (II Kings 14:27)**

Prophets have to resist the pressure of people to give them a word. Some feel that if they do not always have a word to deliver then there is something wrong. This is a sign of immaturity in ministry. A prophet is known by what he does not say rather than by what he says. If a prophet is always talking, when is he listening?

*V. Prophets cannot be wrong.*

`Paul told the Corinthians to judge the words given, even by prophets. In both Testaments, prophetic revelation was judged. True prophets may error if they prophesy for gain or out of their own opinions. Some prophets are deceived into thinking they cannot be wrong.

Some feel to admit that they can be wrong will render their ministries invalid. However, the prophet who walks in the understanding that he can be  wrong is seldom, if not ever wrong. This is because he is walking in humility.

The grace of God rests upon the humble.

Humble prophets will not fail in their ministries. God's grace will cover them as they minister the word of the Lord.

> *But the prophet, which shall presume to speak a word in my name, which I have not commanded him to speak, or that shall speak in the name of other gods, even that prophet shall die. And if thou `say in thine heart, How shall we know the word which the Lord hath not spoken? When a prophet speaketh in the name of the Lord, if the thing follow not, nor come to pass, that is the thing which the Lord hath not spoken, but the prophet hath spoken it presumptuously: thou shalt not be afraid of him. (Deuteronomy 18:21-23)*

> *Let the prophets speak two or three and let the other judge. (I Corinthians 14:29)*

*VI. Prophets cannot operate in other offices.*

A prophet can operate in another ministry office. We find that Samuel was a priest, prophet, and judge. Moses was a prophet and shepherd of Israel and Deborah was a prophetess and judge. David was also a prophet. He is remembered for being Israel's greatest king.

However, the Psalms are full of prophecies that reflect the prophetic ministry of David. When Peter delivered his first sermon, he reminded the Jews that David was not only a great king, but also a prophet.

> ***Men and brethren, let me freely speak unto you of the patriarch David, that he is both dead and buried, and his sepulchre is with us unto this day. Therefore being a prophet, and knowing that God had sworn with an oath to him, that of the fruit of his loins,***

*according to the flesh, he would raise up Christ to sit on his throne; He seeing this before spake of the resurrection of Christ, that his soul was not left in hell, neither his flesh did see corruption. (Acts 2:29-31)*

Knowledge of the office of the prophet is important to understanding the work of Christ in the Church. Illumination helps to develop an appreciation for this ministry and a desire to see it in operation along with the apostles, evangelists, pastors, and teachers.

# 7

# *False Prophets*

There is still much to be learned about the prophetic office. However, understanding comes with responsibility. The Church has to stand against deception. The scriptures are clear that the number of false ministers will increase as the end of this age approaches. Not every individual preaching in the name of the Lord is His servant.

The enemy seeks to destroy the work of God in the earth through imitation. Therefore, the enemy sets his false ministers in the Church to undermine the work of God's chosen vessels. False ministers are here, but the saints are not to be afraid of falling into deception. False ministers provide a service to the Church. How?

*For there must be also heresies among you, that they which are approved may be made manifest among you. (I Corinthians 11:19)*

When Paul used the word heresies, he was speaking of divisions and those that caused them. False ministers seek to keep the Church in perpetual dissension and division. Their ministries put enmity between believers with the intent to create a following for themselves.

The answer to "How do false ministers provide a service to the Church?" seems non-existent. However, the statement of Paul provides a simple explanation. False ministers help us to recognize true ministers of God.

Paul said that there must be heresies (and those that cause them) among you so that those who are approved (right, true, anointed, etc.) might be made visible. The ministries of false ministers demonstrate to the Church the improper way to minister. Therefore, when true ministry is in operation, it can be received without fear.

## Recognizing False Ministers

We cannot end our discussion of prophets without discussing false prophets. Before examining false prophets exclusively, it is imperative that we are able to recognize the characteristics of any false minister (or layman). Jesus gave this warning concerning false ministers.

> *Beware of false prophets, which come to you in sheep's clothing, but inwardly they are ravening wolves. Ye shall know them by their fruits. Do men gather grapes of thorns, or figs of thistles? Even so every good tree bringeth forth good fruit; but a corrupt tree bringeth forth evil fruit. A good tree cannot bring forth evil fruit, neither can a corrupt*

*tree bring forth good fruit. Every tree that bringeth not forth good fruit is hewn down, and cast into the fire. Wherefore by their fruits ye shall know them. (Matthew 7:15-20)*

One true way to recognize false ministers is by the fruit that they bear. Fruit refers to their lifestyles and not their ministries. Moreover, not everyone that is false calls himself an apostle or prophet. Though false prophets exist, there are also false evangelists, pastors, and teachers. Regardless of the title that a false minister has, he (or she) will exhibit the following characteristics.

**They preach that godliness is gain.** Godliness to false ministers means prosperity and healing. They seldom teach against sin. They promote serving God for what you can get.

*If any man teach otherwise, and consent*

*not to wholesome words, even the words of our Lord Jesus Christ, and to the doctrine which is according to godliness; He is proud, knowing nothing, but doting about questions and strifes of words, whereof cometh envy, strife, railings, evil surmisings, perverse disputings of men of corrupt minds, and destitute of the truth, supposing that gain is godliness: from such withdraw thyself. (I Timothy 6:3-5)*

They only teach that you belong to God and should have the best. They promote the concept that God only wants you blessed, without declaring that God also wants character, integrity, and holiness in His people. Their doctrine focuses on the miraculous work of God and His blessings, exclusively. They promote God's blessing, rather than God and His Christ. They teach individuals how to prosper in God without living for Him.

They were once servants of God. Many false ministers have genuine conversion experiences. They entered ministry by the call of God. However, consistent rebellion, sin, pride, and greed caused them to error from the truth.

> *For if after they have escaped the pollutions of the world through the knowledge of the Lord and Saviour Jesus Christ, they are again entangled therein, and overcome, the latter end is worse with them than the beginning. For it had been better for them not to have known the way of righteousness, than, after they have known it, to turn from the holy commandment delivered unto them. But it is happened unto them according to the true proverb, the dog is turned to his own vomit again; and the sow that was washed to her wallowing in the mire. (II Peter 2:20-22)*

Peter wrote that false ministers did escape the pollutions of the world by Christ. However, they returned to their sins and filthy ways. Consequently, Peter added, they are worse than they were before their initial conversion. It serves as a warning to every minister. If the love of money, pride, and sin are not rejected, the road to becoming an enemy of God becomes inevitable.

**Recognizing False Prophets**

False prophets will demonstrate the same behavior as other false ministers. However, there will be certain traits that readily visible in false prophetic ministers.

**They prophesy for money.** False prophets will always include money in their ministry. No matter the topic or subject, it will end up on money. They will twist scriptures to manipulate the people into giving to them.

Remember:

NO PROPHET OF SCRIPTURE EVER ASKED FOR MONEY OR REWARD TO GIVE A PROPHETIC WORD.

They will tell you to give in order to "seal" the prophetic word for personal gain. We should give to ministers that have blessed us, but it should never be by their request. We can bless those that have blessed us spiritually.

In the scriptures, they would bring a gift to the prophet because they wanted to, not because he asked or demanded it for ministry. Remember, Elisha declined Naaman's gifts he brought when he came for healing.

**They use witchcraft.** The prophets never used rituals and spells to relay God's message. They only "acted" or demonstrated the prophetic word as the

Lord directed. Beware of prophets that warn you about objects and things without any spiritual basis or insight. When they begin to tell you to use certain oils, water, or cloths to receive a blessing, it is a sign of falsehood or immaturity in ministry.

**They operate in false authority.** False prophets do not operate in godly authority. They establish their own authority in the Body of Christ. They disguise their wickedness by first appearing as true prophets.

> *For such are false apostles, deceitful workers, transforming themselves into the apostles of Christ. And no marvel; for Satan himself is transformed into an angel of light. Therefore it is no great thing if his ministers also be transformed as the ministers of righteousness; whose end shall be according to their works. (II Corinthians 11:13-15)*

Paul stated that those who are false would resemble those who are true. However, once they have gained some respect, they will attack other leaders. The false apostles and leaders of Paul's day tried to defame him and establish their own authority in the churches. False prophets use this tactic today. Through the defamation of others, they exalt their personal ministries.

**They twist the scriptures.** Another tactic used is misinterpretation of scripture to establish authority. They find scriptures that refer to prophetic authority and claim it for themselves. They scare believers into thinking that because they are prophets, they are superior to others.

True prophets will be humble men and women. They will not promote their personal ministries. The authority that they operate in is backed by the power of God and recognized in the Church.

**They operate in counterfeit gifts.** False prophets minister with the wrong motives. Therefore, the Spirit of God withdraws Himself from their ministries. Since false prophets do not recognize the withdrawal of God, they strive to operate in gifts to validate the ministry. They begin to rely on their own human spirit and help from demonic influence to appear spiritual. This happened to King Saul.

*But the Spirit of the Lord departed from Saul, and an evil spirit from the Lord troubled him. (I Samuel 16:14)*

*And it came to pass on the morrow, that the evil spirit from God came upon Saul, and he prophesied in the midst of the house: and David played with his hand, as at other times: and there was a javelin in Saul's hand. (I Samuel 18:10)*

Because of Saul's continual rebellion, the Spirit of God departed from him. An evil spirit replaced God's Spirit. When the evil spirit came upon him, he prophesied. His prophecy came from the wrong source. This eventually happens to false prophets. The Holy Spirit lifts and they use demonic influences to still function.

**They prophesy lies from their imaginations.** False prophets will make up lofty prophetic utterances. They will seem very spiritual, but oftentimes vague in content.

> *I have heard what the prophets said, that prophesy lies in my name, saying, I have dreamed, I have dreamed. How long shall this be in the heart of the prophets that prophesy lies? yea, they are prophets of the deceit of their own heart. (Jeremiah 23:25-26)*

They will give prophecies based upon someone's outer appearance and expression. In addition, they prophesy their own desires. Conversely, because a prophetic word may seem vague, it does not mean it is not from the Lord. The Lord may speak a word in part that the hearer would be drawn into seeking the Lord for clarity.

Though false prophets and ministers exist, believers are not to walk in fear. However, Christians have to be able to learn to recognize false ministers. In addition, the presence of false ministers should give believers a greater appreciation for godly leaders and ministries within the Church.

www.ingramcontent.com/pod-product-compliance
Lightning Source LLC
Chambersburg PA
CBHW020514100426
42813CB00030B/3241/J